mind-stretching math riddles

MATH for All Seasons

BY **Greg Tang**

ILLUSTRATED BY **Harry Briggs**

SCHOLASTIC INC.

NEW YORK TORONTO LONDON AUCKLAND SYDNEY
MEXICO CITY NEW DELHI HONG KONG BUENOS AIRES

A NOTE ABOUT MATH FOR ALL SEASONS

Math for All Seasons is the second in a series of books that teaches problem-solving to children. It is written for children ages 5–8, a slightly younger audience than for *The Grapes of Math*, but it shares the same goal of encouraging kids to think through problems rather than relying on formulas and memorization. This book can also help children make a smoother transition from counting to arithmetic by introducing intuitive ways to group and add numbers.

Math for All Seasons teaches four important lessons in problem-solving. First, kids are taught to be open-minded and to consider many approaches, not just the most obvious ones. Second, they are encouraged to think strategically, by grouping numbers in ways that make adding easier. Third, they are introduced to timesaving methods such as subtracting to add. Finally, kids learn to simplify problems by looking for patterns and symmetries.

In writing *Math for All Seasons*, I want to spark children's interest in math by showing them firsthand how fun problem-solving can be. I hope to inspire them to have confidence in themselves and their ability to think creatively, and, by posing problems in terms of poems and pictures, I hope to present math in a broader, more interesting way. Enjoy!

Greg Tang

BRIGHT BULBS

Canals and bikes and windmills, too,
Grassy fields and skies of blue.

In Holland spring's the time of year
For pretty flowers far and near.

How many tulips are in bloom?
A clever tack you must assume.

Mixing colors is the way
To make a really smart bouquet!

FIND THE ANSWERS AT THE END OF THE BOOK!

RAINING CATS AND FROGS

They say it's raining cats and dogs.
Why not lizards, snakes, and frogs?

Next time the weather's getting wet,
Forget the forecast—call a vet!

Can you count the dots you see?
Try to add them cleverly.

Group them in a special way,
Make sums of ten this rainy day!

SHELL GAME

The sun is rising on the farm,
Cows are stirring in the barn.

The pigs are rolling in the muck,
In the coop the chickens cluck!

How many chicks have hatched today?
Try to find a clever way.

To quickly count this chirping batch,
Subtract the one that's yet to hatch!

EASTER ART

A canvas made of fragile shells,
A palette filled with soft pastels.

Each becomes a painted prize,
A treasure in a child's eyes!

Can you count each work of art?
Here's a hint before you start.

When it's paintings that you view,
Try to think in groups of two!

HOT TIPS

My ice cream's melting in the sun.
It makes a mess before I'm done.

On my clothes are many drips.
Drat these cones with broken tips!

Can you count up all the scoops?
Try to first make clever groups.

Instead of counting row by row,
Simply add the cone below!

MADAM BUTTERFLY

My life has taken quite a turn.
I used to be a lowly worm.

Now I spread my wings and fly—
Look how cool a bug am I!

How many dots adorn these wings?
See what clever thinking brings.

There is a mate for every one,
Make groups of ten and you'll be done!

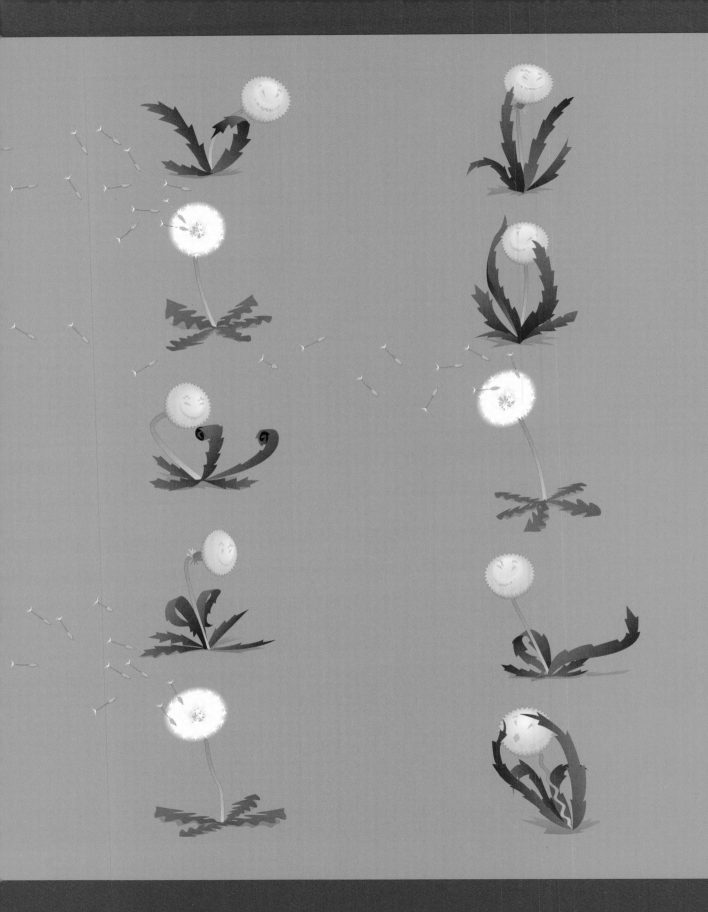

NOT-SO-DANDY LIONS

These lions are a stubborn breed—
There's never just a single weed.

The trouble starts when they get loose,
They catch a breeze and reproduce!

How many plants are still in bloom?
A perfect lawn they're sure to doom.

Count by fives the plants you see,
Then subtract the seedy three!

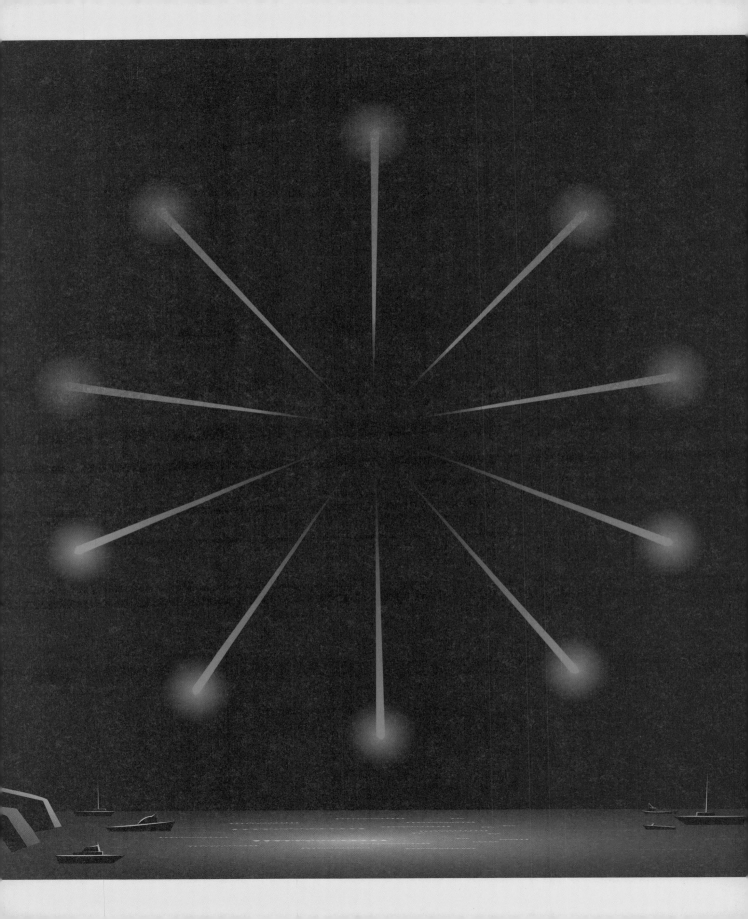

DOUBLE DE-LIGHTS

Waiting is the hardest part.
Please, oh, please just make it dark!

Bursts of color high above,
Booming noises that I love.

Can you count each spark of light?
Here's a way that's really bright.

Instead of counting every one,
Double half and you'll be done!

AMAZING GRAIN

This type of corn is far from plain,
In fact it's wild for a grain.

Brown and gold and sometimes blue,
Even red and purple, too!

Can you count each colored ear?
A smart approach is very clear.

Please consider many ways,
Then add across to solve this maize!

BABY OAKS

A mighty oak—the grandest tree,
Consider what it used to be.

A little acorn on the ground,
A squirrel's prize when it is found.

Can you count the baby oaks?
Here's a trick for all you folks.

When you're adding threes and twos,
Pairs make five and that's good news!

SCARY SQUASH

Ghouls and goblins, ghosts and bats,
Tricks and treats and witches' hats!

Scary creatures in the night,
Jack-o'-lanterns glowing bright.

Can you count each smiling face?
This may help you just in case.

Add the pumpkins, every one,
Subtract the plain ones and be done!

FALL FINALE

Autumn's colors bright and bold,
Orange, red, and lots of gold!

For trees it is the final show.
Coming soon is winter's snow.

Just how many leaves are there?
Find a pattern in the air.

Make groups of five and you will see,
An ending happy as can be!

TEARS FROM HEAVEN

Snowflakes fill the winter sky,
Frozen tears when heavens cry.

Try to catch one on your nose,
A gust of wind and there it goes!

How many flakes are in the air?
Add them all with extra care.

Here's a hint, a little clue,
Tilt your head to see anew!

ICE COLD

Frozen, shiny, glassy spikes,
Tempting treats for little tykes.

"Please don't eat them!" Mother cried.
"Find a clean one," Father sighed.

Can you count each icy treat
Before they've melted in this heat?

Here's a hint to help you count,
The number five's a smart amount!

HOLIDAY SPIRIT

A simple phrase that some believe,
"Better to give than to receive."

The more we share and less we take,
A better world is what we make!

How many presents do you see?
Imagine where a gift could be.

Find the sum including these,
Then subtract them if you please!

HAPPY NEW YEAR

New Year's Eve, the perfect night
To look ahead and make it right.

All the things you've sworn to do—
Now's the time to start anew!

Can you count the party hats?
You can do it just like that!

A group of ten you'll need to find,
Add the rest for "auld lang syne!"

ANSWERS

BRIGHT BULBS

Rather than adding tulips across each row, add down along each column. Since each column has 5 tulips, there are 15 tulips altogether.

$5 + 5 + 5 = 15$

RAINING CATS AND FROGS

When possible, add numbers that have easy sums. The umbrellas can be matched so there are 10 dots in each pair, or 20 dots altogether.

$10 + 10 = 20$

SHELL GAME

First add up all the eggs, including the middle one that hasn't hatched. There are 3 rows of 3 eggs, or 9 eggs altogether. Now subtract the middle egg to get 8 baby chicks.

$9 - 1 = 8$

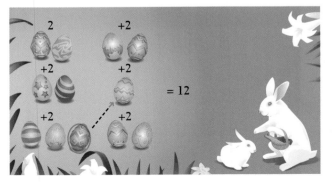

EASTER ART

First imagine moving 1 egg from the group of 3 to the single egg. Now there are 6 groups with 2 eggs each, or 12 eggs altogether.

$2 + 2 + 2 + 2 + 2 + 2 = 12$

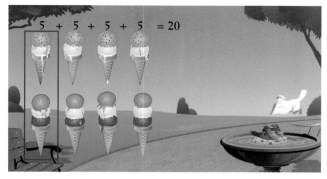

HOT TIPS

Rather than adding scoops across each row, add down along each column. Since each column has 5 scoops, there are 20 scoops altogether.

$5 + 5 + 5 + 5 = 20$

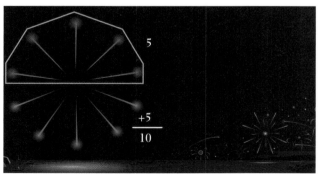

MADAM BUTTERFLY

When possible, add numbers that have easy sums. The butterflies can be matched so there are 10 spots in each pair, or 20 spots altogether.

$10 + 10 = 20$

NOT-SO-DANDY LIONS

First add up all the dandelions, including the seedy ones. There are 2 columns of 5 dandelions, or 10 dandelion plants altogether. Now subtract the 3 seedy ones to get 7 dandelions still in bloom.

$10 - 3 = 7$

DOUBLE DE-LIGHTS

Since the sparks are symmetrical, just count the sparks on one half. Then double this amount to get 10 sparks of light.

$5 + 5 = 10$

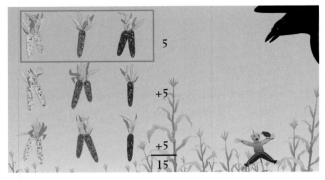

AMAZING GRAIN

Rather than adding ears down along each column, add across each row. Since each row has 5 ears, there are 15 ears altogether.
5 + 5 + 5 = 15

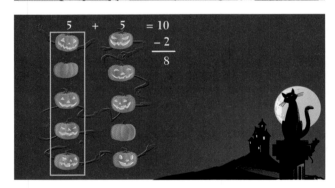

BABY OAKS

When possible, add numbers that have easy sums. The acorns can be grouped to make 3 sets of 5 acorns, or 15 acorns altogether.
5 + 5 + 5 = 15

SCARY SQUASH

First add up all the pumpkins, including the 2 that have not been carved. There are 2 columns of 5 pumpkins, or 10 pumpkins altogether. Now subtract the 2 plain ones to get 8 smiling faces.
10 − 2 = 8

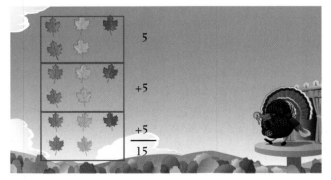

FALL FINALE

Notice there are 5 leaves in the first 2 rows. This pattern repeats itself twice below, so there are 15 leaves altogether.
5 + 5 + 5 = 15

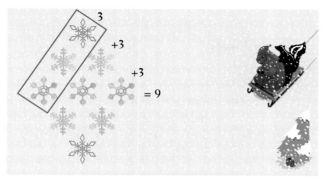

TEARS FROM HEAVEN

Instead of seeing the snowflakes in rows, look along the diagonal to see 3 groups of 3 snowflakes, or 9 snowflakes.

$3 + 3 + 3 = 9$

ICE COLD

When possible, add numbers that have easy sums. The icicles can be grouped to make 2 sets of 5 icicles, or 10 icicles.

$5 + 5 = 10$

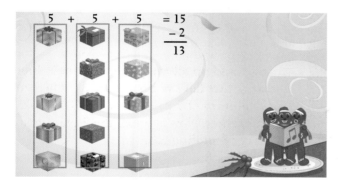

HOLIDAY SPIRIT

First imagine 2 presents where they seem to be missing. Then there would be 3 columns of 5 presents, or 15 presents. Now subtract the imaginary ones to get 13 presents.

$15 - 2 = 13$

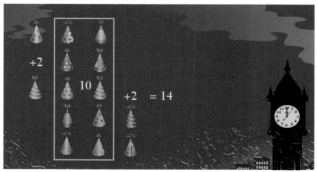

HAPPY NEW YEAR

Find a rectangle consisting of 2 columns of 5 hats each, or 10 hats. Add the remaining 4 hats to get 14 hats altogether.

$10 + 2 + 2 = 14$

SPECIAL THANKS TO STEPHANIE LUCK

FOR HER INSPIRATION, CREATIVITY, AND GOOD CHEER.

This book was originally published in hardcover
by Scholastic Press in 2002.

ISBN-13: 978-0-439-75537-5
ISBN-10: 0-439-75537-9

Text and illustrations copyright © 2002 by Gregory Tang

12 11   11 12 13/0

Printed in the U.S.A.   40   •   First Bookshelf edition, July 2005

The text type was set in 19-point Electra LH Bold.
The display type was set in Countryhouse. Harry Briggs's art was
created on the computer. Book design by Marijka Kostiw